THE ACTION-DRIVEN LIFE

THE ACTION-DRIVEN LIFE

Seven Steps to Finding Your Winning Formula

DON R. VARNEY

iUniverse, Inc.
Bloomington

THE ACTION-DRIVEN LIFE
Seven Steps to Finding Your Winning Formula

iUniverse books may be ordered through booksellers or by contacting:

iUniverse
1663 Liberty Drive
Bloomington, IN 47403
www.iuniverse.com
1-800-Authors (1-800-288-4677)

ISBN: 978-1-4759-5656-6 (sc)
ISBN: 978-1-4759-5658-0 (hc)
ISBN: 978-1-4759-5657-3 (ebk)

Library of Congress Control Number: 2012919925

Printed in the United States of America

iUniverse rev. date: 11/07/2012

CONTENTS

PREFACE

The greatest discovery of any generation is that a human can alter his life by altering his attitude.

—William James, psychologist and philosopher

I believe that everyone has a burning desire to win, but many people anticipate and rationalize defeat before they even compete. I am sure that's because they *believe* they can't win. As I have said for years: If they believe that, they are right! They have defeated themselves by mentally giving up before even trying.

For instance, let's say John and I are going to play tennis. John has always won our previous matches. If I make the assumption that he will win again, in my mind, I have already lost even though the match has yet to begin.

On the other hand, if I decide I will play my best game ever that day, I might just win.

So what is *your* attitude about yourself? Do you have a "losing" mentality or a "winning" mentality?

The ACTION-Driven Life is designed to introduce you to the thought processes I've used to shape my own positive winning attitude.

Adopting a winning attitude can help you live up to your potential. It helped me to become a sales leader, climb the ladder to upper-level management, and eventually establish my own companies. I'm always striving to become the best I can be. The true reward for me is that now I am able to help others do the same.

This book is short and to the point. All I ask is that you keep an open mind while you are reading it.

Who knows what changes may happen to you in your ACTION-driven life.

Enjoy the journey.

Don R. Varney, encourager
San Antonio, Texas

ACKNOWLEDGMENTS

I would like to express my appreciation to the following people:

To my wife, Yvonne, who has been an inspiration in my life. She has always supported my endeavors and is one of the reasons I completed this book.

To all the members of my family for their love, support, and understanding of a little boy's dream. To my grandmother

Maudie McCoy, who always loved me unconditionally. She played a big part in showing me how to judge the character of a person.

To my hot-tea-and-glazed-donut friend, Mr. Pearson, who daily told a little five-year-old boy that he could be anything he wanted to be.

I hope he knows that his words of encouragement have helped me throughout my life.

To the staff of the United States Air Force Recruiting School for showing me how to dream big, set goals, and live a positive life. Their training and challenges changed the course of my life.

To the teachers and coaches who cared enough to show me the right way to work, play, and live. I even have to thank those who told me "that won't work" or "you can't do it," because they stoked the fire in me to succeed.

To Ruben Soto and Cathy Johnson for helping me put my words into print.

Finally, to everyone who has challenged me to live life fully, I thank you.

Chapter 1

ATTITUDE

Always bear in mind that your own resolution to succeed is more important than any one thing.

—Abraham Lincoln, sixteenth president of the United States

Who hasn't heard one of these remarks at some time in his or her life?

"What's wrong with your attitude?"

"You had better change your attitude!"

But you know, "having an attitude" is not necessarily a problem. Too many of us automatically associate "attitude" with "negative," as in *bad attitude*.

I prefer to emphasize the positive. That is, I prefer to think we all have good attitudes, because despite the many problems we encounter in our lives, we still get up and go to school or to work or take care of our families every day. That's positive, not negative.

That positive attitude enables us to keep showing up and trying, even though going to class or work may not be exactly what we want to do at the moment. To me, that perseverance is a positive.

Let me tell you a personal story about how my attitude almost got the best of me.

In 1972, while serving in the United States Air Force, I had the opportunity to attend the USAF Recruiting School. I went straight from the flight line, where I was the noncommissioned officer-in-charge of maintenance training, to the classroom. When it came time for my first classroom test, it was not what I had expected: I was told I had to give an extemporaneous motivational speech the very next morning.

I was petrified. That night in the barracks, I wrote out the speech word for word and tried to memorize it (yes, I realize that is not extemporaneous). I didn't get much sleep, and the next morning I was sweating bullets. In giving the speech, I managed to do everything wrong, and the instructor's evaluation reflected that: "Unsatisfactory performance. See me after class."

After class, the instructor told me, "I suggest you pack your bags; I believe you should quit and go home." I'll tell you, that turned out to be just what he needed to say to someone who's had a competitive attitude his whole life. That competitive attitude kicked in, and I told him, "No, sir, I'm not going home."

In a split second, I turned my attitude around. I knew I was willing to do whatever it took to master public speaking. That decision was the beginning of my speaking career.

Today, when I see a microphone, I get *excited*; I can't wait to speak!

It Is Your Choice

You can have a "Yes, I can" attitude or a "No, I can't" attitude. Let me tell you, I want to have a "Yes, I can" attitude. When people are around me, I want them to leave saying, "I don't know what that guy is doing, but he's one of the most positive guys I've ever met. You know, I don't think that guy has any problems."

Well, we *all* have problems, and we're dealing with them every single day. The difference is in understanding that stress and obstacles and negatives are a part of life, but that we have a choice in how we react to them.

If you get up in the morning hating what you're doing, that's what your day will be all about. But if you get up in the morning and approach your day with a positive attitude, the chances are better that you'll have a good day.

Sure, negatives can creep into your life, but remember that life is a game of small steps that advance you toward your goal. It's a game where *you* have to put it all together. I have used this simple phrase that other positive people use as well: "You can sit around and say 'I can't do that,' or you can say, 'There's nothing I can't do.'" Don't sit back and say, "I don't want to play in the game." Say, "Let's go," and then get out there!

You're Number One

Here's another pitfall you want to step around: Don't fall into the trap of thinking, *Gosh, I'll never be number one.* Maybe you won't be number one in your class or on the basketball court or on the sales team. But you can go home at night, look in the mirror, and say, "You know what? I'm number one *with me* because I'm doing everything within my power to make [your objective] happen. I'm not sitting around saying, 'Golly, I wish I had.' I'm saying, 'I'm glad I did.'"

So What's the Lesson Here?

To build, destroy, or ignore—the choice is yours. Choose to be positive. Choose to build. Get yourself mentally in shape. Create an interest in *yourself*! Invest in *yourself*!

You have the ability to be as great as you want to become. Once you've made a total commitment to yourself, you will not fall short of success. So live up to your potential. And remember:

High Expectations = High Results

Bring out the *champion* in you!

Food for Thought: Attitude

Having an ACTION-driven life requires that you take *action*, so let's get going!

I designed the Food for Thought section at the end of each chapter to nudge you along in the change process and give you something *personal* to take away from the chapter.

Each Food for Thought section contains an action item for you to tackle and questions to help guide your thoughts on the chapter's topic.

You can write down your thoughts here in the book or in a separate notebook. Revisit what you've written occasionally for perspective and to gauge your progress in reaching your goals.

I also include a dessert for you after the Food for Thought section—a photo album.

Here's the action item for chapter 1:

Action

Set aside a time at the end of each day to assess your attitude(s) that day. The time should be a constant—schedule it into your digital calendar or set up a repeating reminder on your smartphone so that you don't forget. Or if you're not into the latest gadgets, stick a note on the fridge door or on your bathroom mirror. The point is, *make attitude assessment a habit.*

Consider keeping a notebook or diary of your assessments. If you find yourself dissatisfied with your attitude in a particular situation, write down what you did and how you could have responded differently. If you notice someone's response—positive or negative—to your attitude, note that as well.

Here are the questions for chapter 1:

Questions

1. Give this question some serious thought and be honest with yourself: "What do I need to change in my attitude? Why do I need to change?"

2. List one or two people you know who have a positive attitude. Why do you consider their attitudes positive? What effect have their positive attitudes had on you?

3. I know you have met or know someone with a negative attitude. What effect did that person's attitude have on you?

You need to release your attitude.

Texas Proud

Attitude in the eye

Auctioneer at a charity event

Study improves
your attitude

Chapter 2

CONFIDENCE

The greatest barrier to success is the fear of failure.

—Sven Goran Eriksson, coach of professional and national soccer teams

Confidence goes hand in hand with a positive attitude.

Think back to your junior high or high school days: Did raising your hand to answer a teacher's question feel as intimidating as jumping out of a plane?

Was it fear of being wrong or making a fool of yourself in front of your peers that held you back?

We all know that teens aren't the only ones who experience a lack of confidence; we adults do, too. Consider how you would react if you were asked right now to stand up and give a speech to a crowd of people. If you are like most people, you'd be petrified.

Just Do It Afraid

When I was a kid, diving was a really big deal at the local pool one summer. The kids who could do flips and twists really impressed all the gang. I wanted so badly to do a flip from the diving board, but fear caused me to *think, think, think* about it but never actually do it. Every day I would get up on the diving board thinking about doing a flip and then change my mind.

I recall the horrors I put myself through until the day I finally just said to myself, *You can do this*. I jumped up, ran to the end of the board, and threw myself in the air, flipping like crazy. It had to be one of the worst flips in the history of diving, but the bottom line is that I faced my fear and did it. Oh, by the way, it really stung when I hit the water.

So many times, if we are willing to go through a little pain to do something we fear, we win great rewards. Just so you know, I still don't do flips at the pool, but I know I could if I had to. A friend of mine said this once, and it stuck with me: "Don't try to overcome your fear before you do something. Rather, Just do it afraid and get it behind you."

It is a wonderful feeling to conquer a fear—suddenly, your confidence soars! You feel like a different person, that you can take on any challenge.

Facing the diving board was one of the clearest examples of that for me.

Remember your first attempt at riding a two-wheeled bike? I remember mine! My older sister was pushing me on the two-wheeler and then let go. She was laughing and having a great time; I was screaming, crying, and doing everything I could not to fall off the bike.

Yet, how do I feel about riding a bike now? I don't think twice about getting on a bike and pedaling down the street—and you probably don't either. But if we hadn't faced that initial fear, we wouldn't be able to reap the benefits of fun and good health we get from riding today.

Jim Brown, a former player for the Cleveland Browns football team, said that he never looked over his shoulder when he was running with the ball. He never worried about who was chasing him. Every time he got that ball, he was confident he was going to score a touchdown. And when you watch old films of him running, that's exactly what he did. The confidence that we will make it happen is what so many of us need to cultivate. Dallas Cowboys defensive tackle Bob Lilly, number 74 and a Football Hall of Fame inductee, told this story: "I was a spindly kid from Throckmorton, Texas, and didn't aspire to play professional football. In fact, I almost didn't play football at all after my junior high football coach knocked me silly while demonstrating a forearm block. I had to have the confidence to pick myself up off the ground and made the decision to give it one more try."

This was a move that changed his life, and arguably the game of professional football, forever. Remember to always keep your eye on the goal and to pick yourself up and to give it one more try.

Confidence is self-sustaining because the more you try what you are afraid of, the more confidence you build. The people you deal with regularly will notice a difference. They may not realize what it is that's different, but they will notice.

So What's the Lesson Here?

Today, do something you've thought about doing but have kept putting off because your fears have held you back. Today is the day. The worst that can happen is it won't work—and if it doesn't, try again! You know that old saying, "If at first you don't succeed . . ." Well, it's true. First attempts often aren't successful, but if you refuse to let fear of failure become a stop sign on your road to success, you will reach your goal.

Action

Do something you are a little uncertain about doing: Take a public speaking class, join a softball league, take dancing lessons . . . you get the idea. As you go through the experience of tackling something new and completing it, keep a diary of your thoughts and confidence levels.

Questions

1. What role does your confidence level—when it's low and when it's high—play in your life?

2. What are you afraid to do? What is making you afraid? Would you be able to go ahead and do it afraid?

3. If you know someone who lacks confidence, what could you do to help that person become more confident? How would it make you feel to know you helped that person?

To Stand and Speak

I Know I Could Do It

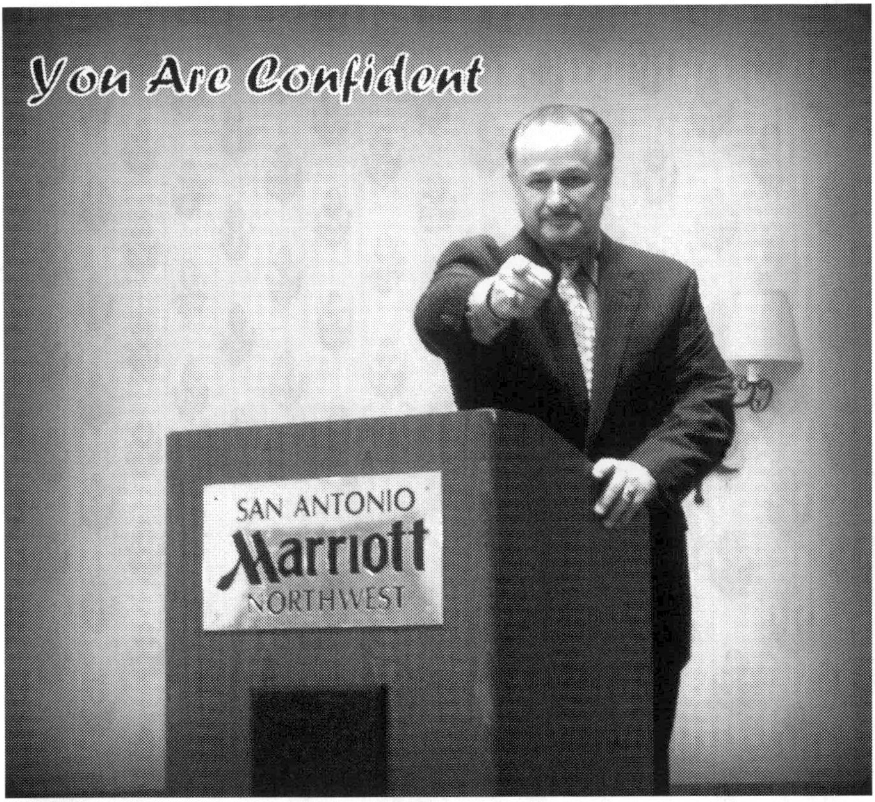
You Are Confident
SAN ANTONIO
Marriott
NORTHWEST

Confidence comes
from Belief in yourself

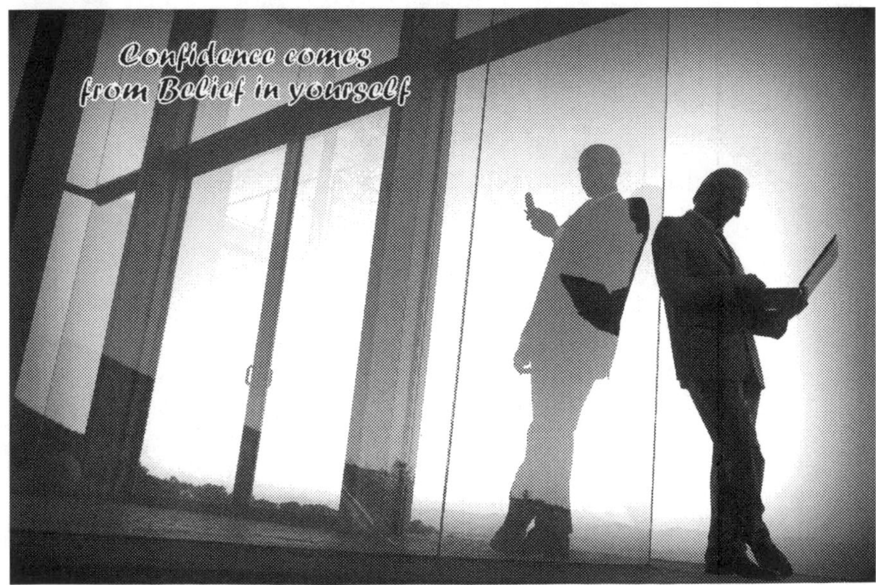

A Smile gives you the
Appearance
of Confidence

Chapter 3

TRAINING

Take the attitude of a student, never be too big to ask questions, never know too much to learn something new.

—Augustine "Og" Mandino, author of
The Greatest Salesman in the World

Training: activity leading to skilled behavior

To train: to become proficient through instruction and practice

"I don't need training."

"I know my job as well as anyone."

"I doubt if there's anything you can teach me. I've been doing my job for years!"

Sound familiar? If it does, it's probably because many of us have felt that way when a training opportunity arrives. The sad part is that the ones who claim they don't need training may need it the most. How do I know that? Because I've been there, but fortunately I came to realize that my concept of training was limited.

Today, I like nothing more than to have someone say to me, "Don, I want to talk to you about something. I think maybe we can do this better." At one point in my life, I might have responded, "You know, I've been doing this for twenty-five years, and I don't think a young person like you can teach me anything." But now I say, "Sit down. You think you've got a better way to do it? Let's hear it."

Remember what I wrote in the preface about keeping your mind open? Now is the time to do just that in regard to training.

Stealth Training

My take on training is that the best possible training occurs when a person doesn't realize he or she is being trained.

Here's an example: Bob's and Jennifer's jobs require them to call prospective customers to set up face-to-face appointments. Bob notices that his coworker Jennifer is not getting any appointments despite her calls, and he strikes up a conversation that goes something like this:

Bob: I noticed you've been making a lot of calls without setting up too many appointments.

Jennifer: Yeah, today I've made ten calls and set up nothing.

Bob: I know what you mean. I was having the same problem.

Jennifer: Was having? Are you having any success now?

Bob: Well, I'm not a hundred percent sure, but I think Fred's idea is really beginning to work. I've made three appointments today.

Jennifer: Fred's idea? (Notice Jennifer is not defensive but interested.)

Bob: Yes. He noticed that I'd been asking prospects if I could come by at a specific time. But they were always busy and said no. Isn't that what's going on with you?

Jennifer: Yeah, they always have a reason for putting you off, don't they?

Bob: Not as much now that I'm using Fred's idea.

Jennifer: Oh? Tell me about it.

Bob: He said to offer a choice, such as Monday or Tuesday, morning or afternoon, two or four p.m.? If you offer only one option, they often turn you down, but if you give them a choice, they are more likely to choose one of your options! Try it to see if it works for you.

Whether or not Jennifer recognizes it, she just received training. It's the kind of training I like to see because most people will accept suggestions from a peer.

You may find you do a better job of training someone when you are sitting and talking over coffee. That's because there's no teacher-student power imbalance; you are talking to your friend about work, and you're talking about a new way to do something or how to use a new tool.

For example, a coworker may not want to take an Internet class because he's uncertain if he will be able to grasp the ins and outs of using the Internet and doesn't want to be embarrassed in front of his peers. However, if you show your coworker how to use the Internet on your breaks, he'll be relaxed and more likely to take to using the new tool.

Someone Does Know More Than You Do—Accept It and Use It

You have to be able to accept training in your life if you're going to move forward. You have to be willing to accept that someone out there knows more than you do in certain areas; in turn, you will know more than someone else does about other areas. Share your knowledge and accept the knowledge of others.

As you start pulling more knowledge into what you are doing, you're going to be able to cope with work and life better and, in turn, you will be more valuable to others. That increased knowledge will have a positive impact both financially and personally.

So What's the Lesson Here?

Think of training as learning a new way to complete tasks more efficiently. That efficiency will allow you time and energy to devote to other efforts.

A little knowledge goes a long way, as they say, and you are the one person who can determine how far it will take you. So learn to accept training from a teacher just as you would from a friend. You'll find that training will become your friend as well.

Food for Thought: Training

Remember, having an ACTION-driven life requires that you take *action.*

Action

Start a Top 100 list of skills you would like to acquire or improve your execution of. The skills can be for work or school or simply for sheer pleasure. *Top 100?* you ask. Well, you have the rest of your life! Once you get that list completed and prioritized, find a trainer or coach for the first skill on your list. Or perhaps you'll just need a how-to book or video. Start with learning or improving two skills a year. That should keep you engaged for the next fifty years!

Questions

1. List two tasks—one of which you thought you already knew how to do—that required that you seek training. What was the lesson you learned from each training?

2. List at least two tasks that you taught someone else to do. How did you feel when you saw that person doing what you had taught him or her?

3. Why do you think you should try to learn at least one new thing daily? Remember, it doesn't have to be a big thing, just new.

Helping

Sharing

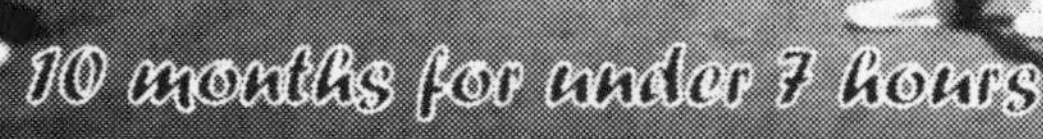

10 months for under 7 hours

Trainng Never stops

Speech Class
San Antonio College

Open communication

Chapter 4

INTEGRITY

Reputation is what others perceive you as being, and their opinion may be right or wrong. Character, however, is what you really are, and nobody truly knows that but you. But you are what matters most.

—John Wooden, UCLA head basketball coach (1948–1975)

It's difficult to maintain total integrity because, let's face it, little white lies tend to slip into our lives daily.

Problems arise when you use such lies to misrepresent yourself—let's say to cover for your mistakes or inadequacies. That kind of lie makes it hard to face yourself in the mirror.

Lying often comes into play during last-ditch efforts to complete tasks while under pressure or time limits. You might feel that your job, a promotion, or something else important is at stake. Funny thing is you may tell a little white lie with no intention to hurt anyone, but it may end up hurting *you*. Exercise integrity to begin with and you won't have to worry about *anyone* getting hurt.

"You've got to trust me on this . . ."

When I hear someone preface his or her remarks with "Believe me" or "Trust me," or if I hear a person ask, "Would I lie to you?" warning flares go up, telling me to be on the lookout for trouble ahead.

Why would someone feel the need to ask "Would I lie to you?" unless that person feared you thought he or she would? At that point, the person has lost me because I am now going to doubt everything I hear.

I was a car salesman at one point in my life, and I would literally cringe every time I heard one of my peers say something along the lines of "Bob, you and I have been working together on getting you this new car, haven't we? I have been trying to answer all your questions, right? Now, let me be honest with you. I wouldn't lie to you, right?"

I wanted to jump up and say, "Why would you say something like that?" Well, salespeople say things like that because that's accepted practice in sales—and not just in car sales. But that "Would I lie to you?" verbiage has gotten us to the point where it's become a caricature of salesmen, which may be amusing in a comedy sketch but is damaging to the profession. So when I get the opportunity to train salespeople, I always stress what *not* to say.

Drop those phrases from your vocabulary and simply begin by saying whatever it is you planned to say in the first place. You'll discover that when you speak, your words will trigger people's attention, not their suspicions.

Your Word Is Your Bond

If people know you are a person of honor, they know that your word is your bond, and that when you say you're going to do something or be somewhere, they can count on you to follow through.

If you encounter someone whose word isn't his bond, don't pay back a wrong with another wrong. Rather, set a standard of integrity. Be the gold standard for the people who don't understand *(yet!)* the value of honor. Realize there are people out there—including people of influence—who are not modeling honor and integrity. That makes it even more crucial that you set an example.

So What's the Lesson Here?

You may not believe that consistently acting with integrity will make a difference, but it will—your actions will ripple out to your neighbors, your coworkers, your friends, your family, and beyond.

Food for Thought: Integrity

Having an ACTION-driven life requires that you take *action*. Be honest with yourself; here's your action item for chapter 5, Integrity.

Action

Pay attention to the people who are around you on a daily basis. Note what they say that shapes your impression of their honesty or lack of honesty.

Questions

1. Do you feel it is okay to tell little white lies or to stretch the truth a little as a means to get what you want? Why?

2. How do you feel when you find out that someone has been untruthful with you?

Never waiver for
once you do
it is gone forever

Stand Strong in
Your Beliefs

Always guard your words

Love Your Country

Objection or would you consider this an objective

Chapter 5

OBJECTIVES & OBJECTIONS

The greatest pleasure in life is doing what people say you cannot do.

—Walter Bagehot, essayist
and journalist

Objective: something toward which effort is directed; an aim or end of action

Objection: a reason or argument presented in opposition

All of us have objectives, be they personal or professional. As you've probably experienced, more often than not, an objection gets in the way of our meeting an objective.

Do yourself a favor and think of objections as a positive. Why? Because every time you get past one, you will be that much closer to your objective.

There are two kinds of objections: surface and core. Core objections are sometimes masked by a surface objection. To get to the truth, you have to dig below the surface.

Whenever an objection arises, consider it from every angle. Where did the objection come from? Did someone say something, or did it come from within? Is the objection based on fact or fear? Figuring out the answers will give you the mental edge you need to overcome the hurdle.

Setting Objectives

Objectives are motivators, so begin by writing down your objectives. Studies have shown that people who write down their objectives have a much higher chance of reaching them than those who don't.

You begin with the end in mind. Then you plot out your strategy for reaching that end. As part of that strategizing, you might make a list of the possible objections—reasons or arguments from yourself or others—standing between you and your objective.

Good example: Roger Bannister was the first man to run an official sub-four-minute mile. Did you know that before Bannister's sub-four-minute mile in 1954, physiologists thought it was physically impossible for a human to accomplish such a feat? Roger Bannister didn't believe it. He had an objective, and he didn't let objections—even scientists' objections—dissuade him from training to break that barrier.

Now think about that: Bannister had to believe he was capable of accomplishing something he had never done, that *no one* had ever done, and what was widely accepted as not humanly possible. In the same way, you have to believe you can indeed make an impact not only on your life but on the lives of others. Speaking of which, within forty-six days of Roger Bannister's breaking the four-minute-mile barrier, John Landy, another great miler of the time, broke Bannister's record. Later in the year, the two runners competed against each other, and both ran the mile in less than four minutes.

So What's the Lesson Here?

Objections are going to come at you every time you set an objective. You can count on it. People are going to start throwing those barriers in your path—you may throw a few yourself. So be ready. Be aware of the arguments against you reaching your objective, figure out your counterarguments and strategies, believe in yourself, and prepare yourself. You may not break a world record, but you're bound to achieve that objective.

Food for Thought: Objectives & Objections

Remember, having an ACTION-driven life requires that you take *action.*

Action

Make a list of objections that have stopped you from reaching an objective. Remember that this may include people who told you it will never work. Be specific.

Questions

1. What hurdles have you overcome, and how did you do it?

2. Look at your list of objectives for your life. What is the most important item on your list? If you don't have such a list, do you think it is a good idea to start one? Why or why not?

There are rewards
when you overcome

Set Clear Objectives

Take a little me time

Be strategic to
overcome obstacles

Chapter 6

NEGATIVES

If I have a thousand ideas and only one turns out to be good, I am satisfied.

—Alfred Nobel, inventor of dynamite
and founder of the Nobel Prizes

I used to be one of the most negative people you would *n*ever want to meet. Until 1972, that is. That's when I attended a school that opened up my mind.

I spent eight weeks at a United States Air Force school learning how to be positive. Most people are surprised when they hear that. "A military school taught you to be positive?" You bet it did. It was one of the most positive times in my life, and it turned my whole way of thinking around.

When I returned to my hometown from that school, people who had known me in the past didn't recognize me. That's how radically the training changed my life.

Replacing a Negative with a Positive

There are an infinite number of negatives to deal with in everyday life: small things like traffic jams, a parking-lot ding in your car door, an hour's wait to see your doctor . . . and on and on. Let's face it: we can't control every situation. What we can control, however, is our reaction.

Don't let negatives rule your day. Recognize when a situation is not "fixable" (at least, at that moment) and keep going. Keep your reactions in check, and make the best of a bad situation. Be positive, and others around you will most likely follow your lead.

How can you make the best of a bad situation? Well, it often takes a little forethought. Good example: Carry an audio book in your car. If you are caught in a traffic jam, slip that CD into your audio system and listen to a book you wouldn't have had time to read otherwise. Same idea when you go to the doctor's office. Your wait won't seem long if you've brought along some task, such as making out a to-do list for the next day, or something pleasant to do while you're in the waiting room. Or use that time to simply relax, breathe deeply, and clear your mind. Great for relieving stress!

Start thinking of solutions to negatives *before* they happen. Something as simple as carrying an extra pen can help you avoid the frustration of having a pen run dry in the middle of an important meeting. Write down all the little negatives that can intrude on a good day. Why? Because once you have identified them, it is so much easier to prevent or work around them.

Don't Waste Your Time with Negative People

I don't have time to spend more than ten to fifteen minutes of my day talking about (or listening to) negatives. When I am in a conversation with people who are being negative and they persist in that negativity, I simply say, "I have to go." It may not be the most socially acceptable solution, but I've done it.

If I'm with someone who's having a massive pity party—and I'm not talking about someone who's truly suffering but rather the person who tells the same stories to anyone who will listen, like the "I didn't get the promotion because my boss doesn't like me" type—I attempt to steer that person into more positive territory by asking about something I know is going well in his or her life or by talking about something positive that's happening in mine. If that approach isn't successful, I ask if we can change the subject.

If, in return, Negative Nan or Negative Ned later says something negative about you—"He's so positive, it makes me sick"—someone will probably defend you, although you may never know it. Consider that the next time someone says something negative about someone you know. Counter the negativity with a positive statement—it's called "paying it forward."

Turning Stress into a Positive

Stress is a part of life. But too much stress and not having the skills to cope with it can undermine your productivity at work and school and eventually undermine your health.

For me, exercise is a great stress reliever. I contend, however, that you don't have to run five miles a day or play three sets of tennis to reap the stress-reducing benefits of exercise. Moderation and consistency are the keys here. Make exercise part of your daily routine: Get up from your desk every hour and do some stretches, or take the long route to get to the coffee-break room. At lunchtime, take a brisk walk to recharge for the afternoon, and in the evening, take a leisurely walk to unwind.

Incorporate some relaxation techniques into your daily routine as well. If you feel on edge or pressured, close your eyes for a moment or two and breathe deeply. As you exhale, imagine letting the stress go as your breath leaves your body, just like the pressure relief valve on a pressure cooker lets off steam.

If anyone asks you what you're doing, just say you're taking the opportunity to relax for a moment and regroup. Ask that person to join you!

Don't let stress defeat you. Instead, you be the winner. Everyone around you will be better for your victory.

So What's the Lesson Here?

Remember, you are the decider of your emotions and your life.

You can choose to be happy or choose to be sad.

You can choose to be negative or choose to be positive.

Choose to be *positive*!

Food for Thought: Negatives

Having an ACTION-driven life requires that you take *action*. Below is the action item for this chapter.

Action

I believe you should have a positive affirmation for your life. Your task is to write one that depicts you and your goals.

Here's an example of one I use daily:

Today I will have a positive impact on someone's life. I will give someone information that will help her or him become a better person. Why? Because I am a positive person who shares.

Questions

1. What is the one thing you would change in your life for the better, and how are you going to do it?

2. Are there certain situations that can set you off in a negative way? Give this some thought, identify those situations or circumstances, and explain why you react negatively.

3. What can you do on a daily basis to begin putting more positives into your life? When are you going to start, and how do you feel it will affect your life?

Relaxation helps overcome negatives

A positive attitude
always trumps negativity

Always seek counsel in
negative situations

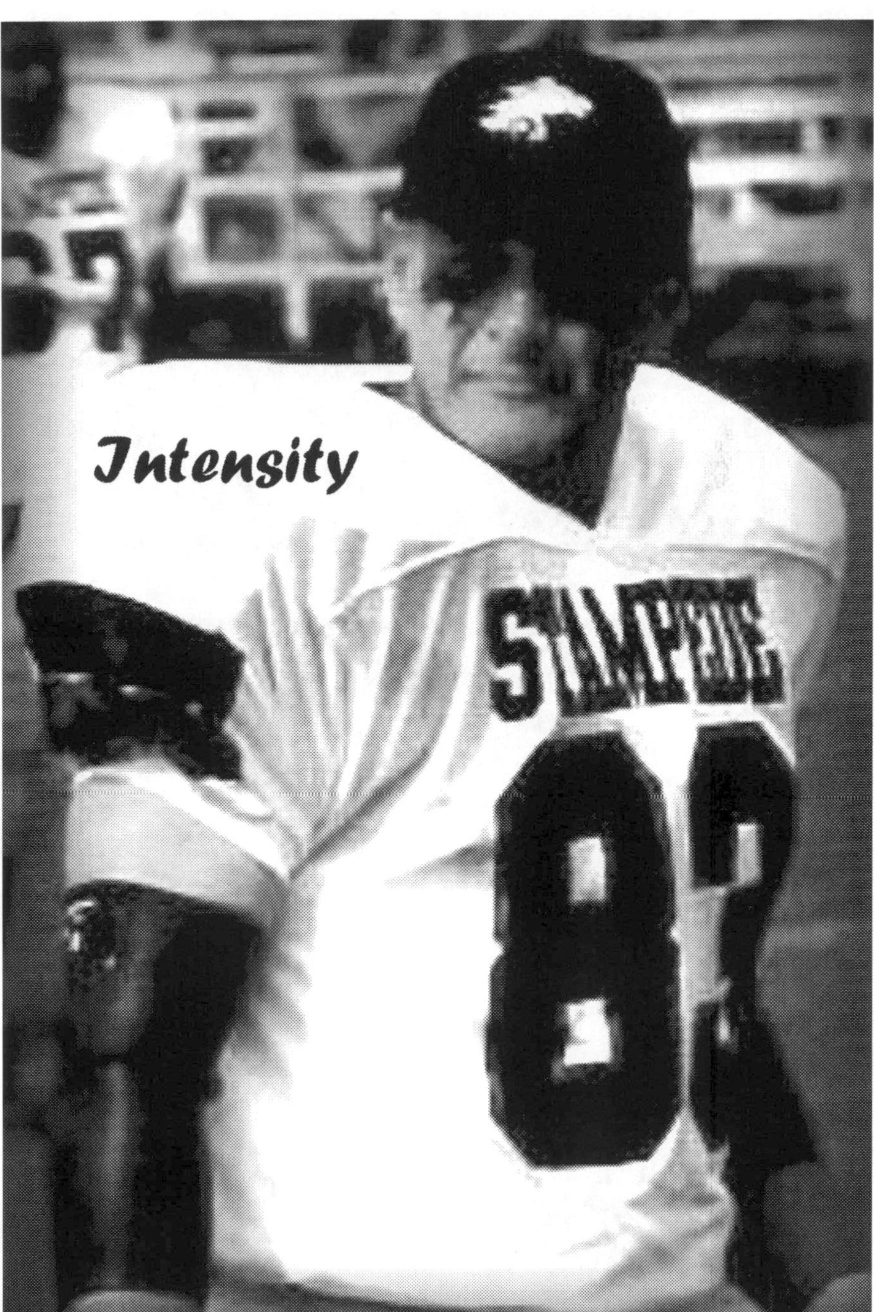
Intensity
STAMPEDE

Knowledge overcomes negatives

Preparation overcomes negatives

Chapter 7

THE SOLUTION

Act as if what you do makes a difference. It does.

—William James, psychologist
and philosopher

I told you in the preface that this book would be short and to the point! We're at the end. Take another look at the titles of the six chapters you've just finished. Combining the first letter of each chapter title gives you the solution to your ACTION-driven life.

Attitude
Confidence
Training
Integrity
Objectives & Objections
Negatives into Positives

You must *act* to change your life. Reading about changing your life and thinking about changing your life are all well and good . . . as preparation. But along with attitude, confidence, training, integrity, objectives, and turning negatives to positives, ACTION is the key.

Your life *is* important, and because of that, your time is important, which is one of the reasons this book is short and to the point. So in closing, I offer my time-management solution, which is also short and to the point. I believe there are only two categories in life: *must do's* and *nice to do's*. You choose.

I also believe daily planning is essential for maximizing daily productivity. Whether you use an elaborate day planner, a smartphone app, or a simple piece of paper, write your to-do actions down according to schedule and/or priority. At day's end, check the list to ensure you've done everything you planned to do, and then set up your list for the next day.

So What's the Lesson Here?

To repeat, the lesson is ACTION: cultivate a positive attitude and confidence, acquire training to boost your ability to make your goal, live with integrity, set objectives and handle objections, and turn negatives into positives.

Now that you have the solution, use it to explore and enjoy the many mysteries of your life. Change what you can, accept what you cannot change, be considerate of others, and get along with your life. If you do, you'll be happier with yourself, and everyone you meet will be happier as well.

We forget that every good that is worth possessing must be paid for in strokes of daily effort. We postpone and postpone until those smiling possibilities are dead. By neglecting the necessary concrete labor, by sparing ourselves the little daily tax, we are positively digging the graves of our higher possibilities.

—William James, psychologist and philosopher

Food for Thought

Remember, to bring out the champion in you, you must take ACTION!

Action

What action are you willing to take to change your life, and why? Map out a plan to accomplish that action. It is important to consider past objectives that were important to you but that you didn't reach. Remember, if at first you don't succeed, try and try again.

Questions

Here are the last questions and some heart-felt requests from me to you:

- Take ACTION!
- Where are you now in regard to achieving your goals?
- Where do you want to be?
- When do want to achieve your goals?

- What are you doing right to reach your goals?
- What do you need to change to reach your goals?
- What are you willing to change to reach your goals?
- Set priorities to accomplish these goals but remember that you may change these priorities at any time.
- Have a great time with your life, and finally . . .
- *Enjoy your life!*

Charlie Ward
Heisman Trophy Winner

Tully Blanchard
Pro Wrestler

Dave Rocker and Friends

Jack Murf the Surf Murphy

Dennis Conner
Captain
Stars and Stripes
Racing Yacht

FCA San Antonio
Golf Marathon

Carrying the Olympic Torch

Derek Anderson
NBA Charity
Event

A pro wrestler
at Derek's event

Josh Davis
Olympic
Gold Medalist
Swimmer

San Antonio Spurs
George Iceman Gervin
&
Johnny Moore

Tommy Kramer
QB
Minnesota Vikings

Dick "Lefty" O'Neal
Negro league pitcher

Jesse James Leija
Boxing Champion

Coach Larry Coker

Afterword

HANDLING ADVERSITY

I have been active all of my adult life. People called me "Iron Man." I was the guy about whom people would say, "If I can do what you do when I'm your age, I'll be happy."

Well, in 2011, all that changed.

It began with pain in my knees. As I began to try to figure out how to stop the pain, the pain moved up into my left hip, then into my right hip, and finally into my lower back.

After multiple visits with doctors, after X-rays and MRIs, I began to receive some findings. I had arthritic degeneration in lumbar vertebrae 3, 4, and 5; a herniated spinal disc; spinal stenosis—a narrowing of the canal the spinal cord runs through, which can cause pain and discomfort—and five stress fractures in my knees and hips. Then the question became, what was causing all these problems?

At that point, I might have been a candidate for a pity party. It was decision time: Was I going to see my glass as half-full or half-empty? As of this writing, the great news is that I've maintained my positive spirit. Also, as a Christian, I have placed my trust in my Lord and Savior Jesus Christ, because I believe He has the power of healing and the power to make the body whole again. I also believe that He will lead me to the right place, where I'll meet the right people that can also do His will.

It turns out that I have a vitamin D deficiency and osteopenia, a lower-than-normal bone-mineral density, which explains the fractures in my knees and hips. Vitamin D is required for healthy bones, but one hundred million Americans have a deficiency because their skin is not exposed to enough sunlight each day for their bodies to manufacture vitamin D. Fortunately, vitamin D deficiency and osteopenia are treatable.

My doctor advised me to go on bed rest to help with the healing process. After some negotiation, he agreed that if I used crutches and stayed off my feet as much as possible, he would allow me to get out of bed for a few hours each day to do my consulting work. At this point, I spend about 90 to 95 percent of my day in bed or on the couch in my home. I've set up a small office there so that I'm able to work. Thank goodness for the Internet, laptops, and cell phones.

I want to let you know that there have been a few times when negative thoughts have crept into my mind. I would ask, "Why is this happening to me?" Sound familiar?

I've made the decision that every time I have a negative thought in regard to my medical condition, I'll turn it around, turn it to the positive, and eliminate that negative. It is my choice to begin being thankful that I can continue to work and contribute. It is my choice: positive or negative. I choose positive.

Being positive, I believe I'll have a full recovery. The bottom line is that I'm still able to move around, still able to make things happen.

So What's the Lesson Here?

Adversity can hit us without warning. Our ultimate success or failure is determined by how we handle adversity. Do we let it dominate or control us? Do we let it take over our every waking moment? Do we allow it to stop us from being productive people?

If the adversity is physical, your body may be compromised, but you're still in control of your mind. Keep yourself mentally strong, agile, and alert so that you can make—thoughtfully and wisely—all the decisions that will come up regarding your health and related issues.

If you are going through adversity, may I suggest that you write down what you're willing to do on a day-to-day basis to make yourself and your circumstances better?

Ask yourself these questions:

- How am I going to live life now that my situation has changed?
- What am I willing to do not to aggravate my situation?
- What am I willing to do to make my situation better?

So here we are at my ACTION solution again:

Attitude
Confidence
Training
Integrity
Objectives & Objections
Negatives into Positives

Maintain a positive attitude. Be confident that you will recover and that you can do the work required to recover. Allow others to teach you how to best take care of yourself. Set objectives and create a plan to reach those objectives. Follow through on that plan. Don't allow negatives to enter your mind, and when you reach your objectives, set new ones!

"It May Not Be Fast, but It Gets Great Gas Mileage"

Obviously, my life has changed drastically. I have always been a person who enjoyed going to the gym and working out. I went to the gym, on average, three to four times a week. Now I have to use a wheelchair when I need to cover any significant distance.

In February, I flew to Anaheim, California, with one of my clients to work a convention. At the airport, I used a wheelchair to get to and from the gate.

Once we arrived at the hotel and saw the distances required to walk from our rooms to the convention center, we had to make some decisions. I rented a powered scooter, which proved to be the answer to my needs.

I couldn't help but notice how people looked at me when I was using a wheelchair or motorized scooter. I decided to be positive and uplifting about my circumstances. I wanted to see how people engaged with me and have a little fun along the way.

The elevator was a good place for me to try out my plan. My opening line was, "They wouldn't give me the 'Flame package,' which is why this is kind of a plain ride. No frills." People always laughed and opened up. My showing a positive spirit helped them deal with my being on a scooter.

Some other lines I used:

- I rent this out by the minute—interested?
- I bet you wish you had thought of this idea!
- Want to race? (Said to others using a scooter; all replied yes and smiled.)
- Will this help me get to the front of the line?
- I forgot my handicap tag; can I park here?
- Has anyone seen an electrical outlet?
- It may not be fast, but it gets great gas mileage.

It was amazing to see the smiles and hear the laughter once they realized I wanted to have fun not sympathy. This proved to me that you can improve any situation with positives and enthusiasm.

And That Lesson Again?

So what is it I hope you learn from my story?

- Be happy with your life regardless of adversity.
- Take care of your body.
- Take care of your mind.
- Stay positive no matter what the situation.

And remember: Take ACTION in your life!

A Good News Report

On May 24 the results from my last MRIs came back, and my doctor was surprised but happy to let me know the stress fractures were healing, which now takes surgery off the table. I will have to maintain bed rest for three months and then start rehab. I am so happy that the power of prayer, positive thoughts, and positive attitude are working.

Remember, only you ultimately choose how to handle adversity.

Don R. Varney

ABOUT DON VARNEY

As my parents made their way to the hospital in Huntington, West Virginia, in April 1946, they didn't have a boy's name chosen for their soon-to-arrive third child. Having had two daughters, my folks thought their chances of having a baby boy weren't that good, but at the last minute, my dad came up with a boy's name—just in case. The hosts of my dad's favorite radio show were two guys named Donald and Richard, and later that day, Donald Richard Varney joined the Varney family. Coincidentally, many years later, Donald Richard would host his *own* radio talk show in San Antonio, Texas.

I don't remember much about my early years, probably because I was born with bronchial asthma and spent most of those years in bed at home or in the hospital under an oxygen tent. In essence, as a small child, I was trapped by asthma.

During that period, my family moved from Huntington to Fort Worth, Texas, where my brother was born. He was a "blue baby," his death caused by a congenital heart condition that today can be easily surgically repaired. His loss, which must have been so tough on my parents, was never discussed in our home.

In the late 1940s, my family moved to Baltimore, Maryland. We lived with my grandparents in the inner city near the docks. My grandmother had a blue-collar restaurant, and the entire family lived on the two floors above the restaurant. The house was a row house—a typical inner-city building that was narrow and deep. My grandparents lived on the second floor, where there was a common living room; my parents slept in the back portion of that floor. My sisters and I had our bedrooms on the third floor.

I have fond memories of that time, that neighborhood, and my grandmother's restaurant. Our neighbors were a lumber company, a corner bar, a small metal shop, and a bread company. So many different cultures surrounded us. Our neighborhood bordered Little Italy—my godparents were Italian, and when we visited their store, we'd eat spaghetti and meatballs—and we also had Irish, Polish, and German neighbors, just to name a few.

It was a different America than most know today. I remember women scrubbing the white marble steps that led up to the stoop, or porch, in front of their doors, women in aprons, guys in their work uniforms (Lee pants and shirts), police twirling their nightsticks as they patrolled the neighborhood.

It was a time when windows and doors were always open—no air-conditioning—and the smells of the different cultures blended in the air. Aromas wafted from the homes and the local bakery and restaurants around us. If you have never had the pleasure of smelling bread being baked, you have missed something so simple but so wonderful. What a memorable aroma stew came alive every morning in that part of Baltimore. Truly, it was a magical time in a young boy's life.

My grandmother's restaurant was no different, because she would bake and cook every morning—always wearing an apron—and the people walking by would follow their noses into the restaurant with a smile on their faces.

The people of that neighborhood and those who came into my grandmother's restaurant helped me to relate well to people regardless of race or circumstance the rest of my life. In my grandmother's restaurant, all were welcome. Her rules were quite simple: if you can pay, you are welcome.

My grandmother also had a reputation for helping those who were down on their luck. Although it was never mentioned, I believe she must have had her own struggles during the Depression. As I watched her give to those who asked her for help, she was teaching me by example to be kind and giving.

The small-business owners, the policemen and firemen, and the workers who surrounded me at the restaurant were the people helping to build America, but, without their realizing it, they were also helping to build a young boy's character.

Of course, I also met people who were not living up to their potential: drunks, criminals, and the like. I felt sad for them, but my grandmother made me realize they were capable of changing their situations. "A person trying to work doesn't have time to get into trouble," she would say.

Every morning, Mr. Pearson, a black man who worked as a security guard at one of the plants in the neighborhood, came to my grandmother's restaurant to have a cup of hot tea and a glazed donut with his friend.

Mr. Pearson always looked sharp in his meticulously pressed work clothes and shiny boots. He would regularly ask if I would sit with him, and we would talk about all sorts of things. Every time we talked, he would tell me, "Little Governor"—he always called me that—"you can be anything you want to be."

I enjoyed drawing and can remember showing Mr. Pearson my drawings. He always acted interested. I have thought of him often, as he was so kind and offered me positive affirmations for my life. Sometimes I wonder why he was there and why he showed an interest in a sick little white kid. He certainly didn't have to. He could have come into the restaurant, had his tea and donut, and left, like so many others did every day.

What great times we had talking, drinking tea, and eating glazed donuts. He helped instill in me the concept of living bigger than one's circumstances, dreaming big, and wanting to inspire others as he inspired me.

My sisters and I attended Holy Rosary School. I enjoyed going to school. All of us were good students at that time in our lives. At our school, we wore uniforms. I liked that because we were poor, and everyone dressing alike helped me associate with my peers on an equal level.

Because of my asthma, though, I was mostly an observer when it came to playtime. But I remember the neighborhood games: playing curb ball (an inner-city game loosely based on baseball) with a Pinkie, a rubber ball you tried to bounce in different directions and at different heights. Or climbing walls—your back against one wall and your feet on the other; or playing in abandoned buildings. Sometimes we would go to the pier, where there was a small boardwalk with a carnival atmosphere.

Another strong visual memory from those days is the red-and-white Ford Crown Victoria my grandmother bought. It was the greatest car I had ever seen. I loved the chrome molding across the top.

After a few years, my dad moved us to the suburbs (funny word). Our new neighborhood wasn't really that far from downtown, but to us it was way out of the city.

When we had lived above Grandma's restaurant, my sisters and I had walked just over a mile to school. Now we rode the city bus—what a thrill! It was interesting to observe the people on the bus—not much different from today. Most quietly rode to work and quietly returned home. I always found this sad. I loved it when I met someone on the bus who was excited about his or her life and shared that with me.

Another strong memory: When I was seven, I learned a mother's love truly has no boundaries. When a neighbor kid tried to beat me up, I ran into our house and told my mother. She told me to go back outside and not be afraid, but when I did, I heard the kid's mom yelling at him to go back and beat me up again. My mom heard it too, and she walked outside and then over to the kid's mother. A few words passed between them; then suddenly, they started throwing punches! What was a seven-year-old to do? I do remember my mom seemed to be winning before the woman turned and returned to her house. A little later, the police came to our door and talked to my mother about what had happened. The person who had started the whole incident had taken on the role of victim. Definitely a life lesson there. After that, I never doubted that my mother loved me.

I still had asthma attacks, but not as often, and I began to be able to play with neighborhood kids. I got my first bicycle, and riding it for the first time was the scariest, most thrilling thing I had ever done. What a sense of accomplishment I felt!

Other memories: going to the drive-in movie; bologna sandwiches on white bread with mayo, tomato, and onion; eating at Grandma's on the weekend; my first Dr. Pepper bought from a vending machine; going to Fort McHenry, where the lyrics to "The Star-Spangled Banner" were written, and to Washington, DC, to see the museums.

I don't remember watching TV; at that time in my life, TV was not that important. I *do* remember coming home muddy one day after playing in puddles. My dad, furious at me, told me to go find a switch (a tree branch, for those of you who don't know what a switch is), and I'm sure you know what it was for. I brought him a very thin switch, but my plan didn't quite work out the way I thought it would—a thin switch really hurts!

A few years later, we moved to a different part of Baltimore: a better neighborhood, nicer house, different school, *and* we had a family TV. I remember going to Immaculate Heart of Mary and playing on my first baseball team—we wore red ball caps. I don't remember any of my family coming to the games. Sports were becoming important to me but not to them.

At school, I learned the time-honored lesson that honesty is the best policy when I told my teacher that she had misgraded my test paper and that I should have gotten a B+, not an A. She told me to keep the A for being honest. Wow! That had a huge impact on me!

I remember watching television with the whole family in the living room; that TV did bring us together for a little while. I watched Walt Disney's series about Davy Crockett, and on Saturday mornings, all the boys watched Westerns starring the Lone Ranger and Tonto, Gene Autry, and Lash LaRue. After the shows were over, we would all meet outside as if on cue and play cowboys and Indians. Fun times.

But then, for some reason, things started to change in my life. To this day, I still don't know why.

There was my first cigarette (amazing, isn't it, that the kid who couldn't breathe well because of asthma takes up smoking). Smoking was considered cool. Everyone was doing it. It's amazing what peer pressure can do to you.

And then I let myself be bullied into doing something I knew was wrong: I stole a carton of cigarettes so that my friends and I could smoke. My dad found out and took me back to the store and explained to the manager what I had done. Yes, I did have visions of going to jail, and I was scared "straight" that day. The punishment: ten weeks (one for every pack in the carton) on restriction during my summer vacation. I was quite bitter at the end of the summer because of what I had missed, and that was the beginning of my rebellious spirit.

Other memories from that time: getting a burr haircut with my dad, and meeting my first real hero, Vince (Rocky) Dirocco, my sister's boyfriend, who was a football player, a smoker, and a tough guy. I wanted to be just like him.

In 1957, my family moved to Miami, Florida. I have mixed emotions about the two years we lived there. A few things do stand out: living next to a snake farm that had a fifty-foot white cobra out front to draw the tourists' attention, and having to redo fifth-grade work because the Miami public school was a year behind the parochial school I had attended in Maryland. At that time, I could not understand how

I could be punished for having done well in school. Good lesson: You don't always get what is right or just.

The rest of my education was a joke: I got by just so that I could play sports. There were problems at home: When I was a sophomore, my parents divorced, and life seemed, in a word, blurry. I lost focus, even with sports.

I was more interested in knowing when the next party was and who was going to be there. I started believing that it was always someone else who got the breaks. I was walking through life with an "I don't deserve this" attitude. What a jerk I had become. I was not making great decisions; looking back, I'm still amazed I never tried drugs during this period of my life.

My dad had become a devout Baptist; he never stood a chance with me because I didn't want to hear what I felt was his righteous attitude about Christianity. In my opinion, he definitely was not having fun, and I wanted no part of it. Little did I know that he was getting his life together and would meet a wonderful woman, whom he married. He never wavered in his faith, and when he died in the late 1990s, he was highly thought of in his community. He had great friends who spoke highly of him. I wish I had known that man.

Unfortunately, my father and I had never had a great relationship, and I was turning out just like he said I would: *no good*. After failing my senior year, I moved to Dayton, Ohio, where my uncle and aunt had a hand in making some positive changes in my life. My uncle owned a house that he rented to his nephews. If you broke my uncle's house rules, you were out. Period. No second chances. One of my cousins had not followed the rules and was asked to move out, so there was an opening in the house. I was invited to live there.

The most important house rule was your rent was due on the first of each month, no exceptions. That meant you had to have a job because the others were not allowed to pay your portion of the rent. The rest of the rules were about keeping the house clean and maintained.

The year I lived there went by quickly. My cousins were great in that they accepted me yet held me accountable. We played softball, basketball, and flag football and had a lot of fun. I met Mr. Lyle, the sales manager at Richmond Brothers in downtown Dayton, who taught me some secrets to business success. I still use some of his ideas today.

Last, but certainly not least, that year I graduated from high school with a diploma, not with a GED. It was important to me to do it that way, as everyone thought I would once again take the low road. No one thought I would try to finish school, and when I graduated, no one was there to see it. Humbling, but another step to growing up. Earning my high school diploma required me to work full time and go to school five nights a week for an entire school year. My character building was beginning.

With that goal met, I returned home to decide what my next step would be. The draft was looming, and my going into the military seemed to be the next step. I first joined the Army National Guard but then decided to go on active duty and joined the United States Air Force.

Little did I know at the time the impact that decision would have. I spent a total of twelve years on active duty with the United States Air Force, and it laid the foundation for the rest of my life.

While I was a master instructor at the prestigious Air Force Recruiting School at Lackland Air Force Base in San Antonio, I was involved in creating many sales and public speaking courses and received numerous awards and decorations for instructing a full array of students, from noncommissioned officers to generals.

That background enabled me to become successful in the sales arena once I left the Air Force. In 1984–1985, as a general manager, I led my teams to new sales records, including becoming number one in the nation for eighteen consecutive months. In 1995, I became partner and CEO of a nutritional supplement distribution company and once again put together a business strategy that made our company number one in sales.

In my career, I continued to search for ways to enhance my speaking abilities and to provide insightful as well as creative formats for my presentations. I acted in commercials, industrial films, and several movies and even became a headliner on the comedy circuit.

In addition, I hosted a call-in radio show entitled *Don Varney's Positive World* and hosted *Billboards*, a talk show on KSLR Radio in San Antonio, Texas, for more than ten years.

In the sports arena, I fulfilled a lifelong dream of playing professional football by playing tight end for the San Antonio Stampede, which won the USIFL championship in 1998.

I then became the chaplain and assistant coach for the San Antonio Thunder of the North American Football League and the chaplain for the San Antonio Rampage of the American Hockey League. The Thunder's coaching staff was selected to the NAFL Coaching All-Star List in 2001.

Today, I am involved in several business ventures, including VarneySpeaks Motivational/Inspirational Speaking, Znutrition, and Chiropractic Centers of Texas.

Whether I'm speaking to a large group, in a boardroom, or one to one, my goal is to help my audience find the champion within. Just as people in my past inspired me to reach beyond the ordinary, I strive to inspire those I work with and speak to.

Someone asked me once, "When are you going to retire?" My answer: "Retirement is not on my radar because I love helping people and I don't really consider what I do work."

Grandma's Ford Crown Victoria

Doing studio work

My mother and I

Grandma McCoy
Baltimore, MD

Our home and Grandma's restaurant, Baltimore, MD
This picture is from October 2009.

Instructing at the US Air Force Recruiting School